TAKE TEN YEARS

1930s

This book is to

Published by Evans Brothers Limited
2A Portman Mansions
Chiltern Street
London W1M 1LE

First published 1991
Reprinted 1998
© in this edition 1996

Typeset by Fleetlines Typesetters, Southend-on-Sea
Printed in Spain by GRAFO, S.A. - Bilbao

ISBN 0 237 51663 2

Acknowledgements

Maps – Jillian Luff, Bitmap Graphics
Design – Neil Sayer
Editor – Jean Coppendale

For permission to reproduce copyright material the author and
publishers gratefully acknowledge the following:

Cover photographs – The Hulton Picture Company; Topham;
Popperfoto; The Vintage Magazine Co.

Pages 4 and 5 – Popperfoto, The Vintage Magazine Co, The Hulton
Picture Company; Topham; page 8 – Popperfoto; page 9 – (top) The
Hulton Picture Company, (bottom) Topham; page 10 – (top) The
Illustrated London News Picture Library, (bottom) Topham; page
11 – (left) The Hulton Picture Company, (top) Popperfoto, (bottom)
Topham; page 12 – The Hulton Picture Company; page 14 – (left)
The Illustrated London News Picture Library, (top, bottom left,
bottom right) The Vintage Magazine Co; page 15 – (left) The
Hulton Picture Company, (right) The Illustrated London News
Picture Library; page 16 – The Illustrated London News Picture
Library; page 17 – The Vintage Magazine Co; page 18 – The Hulton
Picture Company; page 19 – The Hulton Picture Company; page 20
– (top, bottom) The Illustrated London News Picture Library,
(middle) The Vintage Magazine Co; page 21 – (left) The Hulton
Picture Company, (right) Topham; page 22 – (left) The Hulton
Picture Company, (right) Topham; page 23 – (left) Barnaby's
Picture Library, (middle, top right) The Hulton Picture Company/
The Bettmann Archive, (bottom right) The Illustrated London
News Picture Library; page 24 – Topham; page 26 – (left) Penguin
Books, (top) The Hulton Picture Company/The Bettmann Archive,
(bottom) Topham; page 27 – Topham; page 28 – The Illustrated
London News Picture Library; page 29 – (left, right) Topham, (top)
The Vintage Magazine Co; page 31 – Topham; page 32 – (top)
Topham, (middle) The Hulton Picture Company/The Bettmann
Archive, (bottom) Associated Press/Topham; page 33 – (left)
Topham, (top right) Barnaby's Picture Library, (bottom right) The
Illustrated London News Picture Library; page 34 – Topham; page
36 – (top left) Colorsport, (bottom left) The Hulton Picture
Company, (top right) The Vintage Magazine Co, (bottom right)
Topham; page 37 – (left) The Hulton Picture Company, (right)
Topham; page 38 – The Hulton Picture Company; page 40 – The
Vintage Magazine Co; page 41 – (top) Topham, (bottom) The
Vintage Magazine Co; page 42 – (left) The Vintage Magazine Co,
(right) Topham; page 43 – The Hulton Picture Company; pages 44
and 45 – The Vintage Magazine Co, Topham, Bill Sharman/Colin
Garratt's Steam Locomotives of the World Photo Library.

TAKE TEN YEARS

1930s

KEN HILLS

EVANS BROTHERS LIMITED

Contents

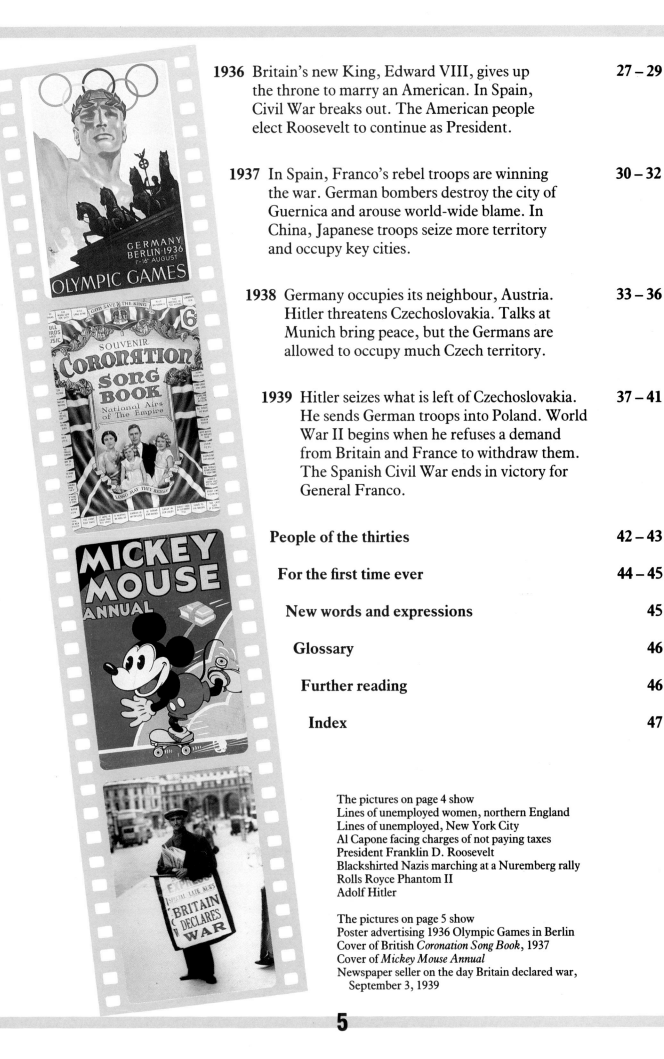

The pictures on page 4 show
Lines of unemployed women, northern England
Lines of unemployed, New York City
Al Capone facing charges of not paying taxes
President Franklin D. Roosevelt
Blackshirted Nazis marching at a Nuremberg rally
Rolls Royce Phantom II
Adolf Hitler

The pictures on page 5 show
Poster advertising 1936 Olympic Games in Berlin
Cover of British *Coronation Song Book*, 1937
Cover of *Mickey Mouse Annual*
Newspaper seller on the day Britain declared war,
    September 3, 1939

Introduction

The First World War ended just over ten years before the thirties began. It had been the most destructive war in history, and it left large parts of Europe in ruins. Slowly during the twenties even those countries which had lost most in the War started to recover. All over the world, living conditions began to improve.

America in the twenties seemed to be entering a golden age. New industries appeared such as the production of cars and motion pictures, and radio programmes developed. Many people grew rich and the American public could afford to spend at a record rate. It looked as though the good times would go on for ever.

As the thirties began, the good times became hard times. America's boom collapsed. The Great Depression, as it was called, spread from America round the world. Businesses were ruined, and millions of workers lost their jobs. They and their families faced a future without hope.

In their misery, the unemployed rebelled. They joined in protest marches. They rioted, and fought the police who tried to stop them. It seemed that law and order was crumbling, even in orderly countries like Britain.

The crisis made governments everywhere re-shape their policies. In the United States, President Roosevelt's New Deal policy gradually led the country back towards prosperity and in Europe, little by little, the nations recovered.

In Germany, Adolf Hitler promised the people simple solutions to their problems. He offered them strong leadership, and armed Germany for war. On the other side of the world, Japan set out to conquer her giant neighbour China. Other nations were too timid or too busy with their own problems to face these threats to world peace. As the thirties ended, countries which had tried to keep the peace prepared most urgently for war. War came, in Europe, in September 1939.

YEARS	WORLD AFFAIRS
1930	Worldwide depression. Tragedy of peasants in Russia. In India, Gandhi defies the British.
1931	Britain in economic crisis. All-party National Government formed to save the nation. Spain becomes a republic.
1932	Franklin Roosevelt elected US President. British jail Gandhi in India. Nazi support grows in Germany.
1933	Roosevelt's New Deal cheers America. Nazis win power in Germany. Reichstag burns down. Spain in turmoil.
1934	Nazis murder Austrian Chancellor. Hitler does away with his rivals.
1935	Hitler scraps the Versailles Treaty.
1936	Roosevelt re-elected US President. German troops enter the Rhineland. Europe's protests ignored.
1937	Chamberlain becomes British Prime Minister.
1938	Germany seizes Austria and threatens Czechoslovakia. A meeting in Munich prevents war.
1939	Germany swallows the rest of Czechoslovakia and threatens Poland. Europe prepares for war.

Introduction

WARS	PEOPLE	EVENTS
	Amy Johnson's historic flight to Australia. Sherlock Holmes' creator dies. Abyssinia's new Emperor, Haile Selassie, crowned.	German Nazis attack Jews. Giant airship *R101* crashes. New planet Pluto discovered.
Japan and China fight in Manchuria.	Inventor Thomas Edison dies. Campbell sets new landspeed record. Scarface Al Capone jailed.	Mutiny in Britain's Royal Navy over pay cuts. Huge earthquake in New Zealand. Slave labour builds Russian canal.
Fighting in Manchuria spreads to China. Japanese officers kill Prime Minister.	George Eastman, inventor of Kodak camera, dies. Amelia Earhart sets Atlantic record.	Los Angeles Olympic Games. Dutch win land from the sea. Sydney's new bridge opened.
	Campbell sets new landspeed record.	Japan and Germany quit League of Nations. Prohibition ends in America. First round-the-world solo flight.
Civil war in China. Nationalists surround Communist Red Army. Border fighting in Abyssinia.	Composer Sir Edward Elgar dies. Death of Marie Curie. German children join movement supporting Hitler.	Giant ocean liner *Queen Mary* launched. Women in shorts at Wimbledon Tennis Championships.
In China the Red Army fights its way to safety. Italians invade Abyssinia.	Allen Lane's publishing revolution. Campbell's new landspeed record. George Gershwin's brilliant new opera.	Nazis ban jazz music. High flying – new altitude record. Britain joins the arms race.
Civil war breaks out in Spain. European powers agree to keep out. Germany occupies the Rhineland. Italians conquer Abyssinia.	Britain's king Edward VIII gives up the throne.	Jesse Owens triumphs at Berlin Olympics. Record Atlantic crossing by airship *Hindenburg*.
Civil war rages in Spain. German aircraft destroy Guernica. Japanese advance in China.	Britain's new king, George VI, is crowned. Joe Louis becomes world heavyweight boxing champion. Composer George Gershwin dies.	German airship *Hindenburg* explodes.
War in Spain goes on. Franco is winning.	America gets a new hero 'Superman'. Disney cartoon success.	Italy wins World Cup at soccer. Night of terror for Germany's Jews. Britain orders 1000 Spitfires.
Franco's victory in Spain's civil war. Germany invades Poland. World War II begins.		British children moved to safety. America's first television programme. First passengers fly the Atlantic.

1930

WORLD SLUMP

WORLD TRADE IN DANGER

June, Washington   President Hoover is increasing taxes on all imported goods. He intends to make foreign goods so expensive that Americans will buy things made in America instead. In reply some countries are threatening to increase taxes on American imports. If many countries do this, no country will be able to sell goods to another and world trade will be strangled.

MILLIONS OUT OF WORK IN USA

Oct, Washington   Three million people are out of work in the United States. Their numbers are rising rapidly. Thousands of businesses are closing down. Over 60,000 workers are losing their jobs every week.

Lines of unemployed people in New York waiting for free food.

BRITAIN'S ECONOMIC PROBLEMS

Oct, London   One and a half million workers in Britain have lost their jobs. The numbers of those out of work grows week by week. Businesses are closing down. No end to the crisis is in sight.

A demonstration by unemployed people in London.

Police and jobless workers clash in London

Oct 15, London   Fighting broke out in the East End of London this afternoon. The scuffles began when police tried to stop out-of-work men marching through the streets to protest about the lack of jobs. The police are preparing for more trouble as the number of those without jobs increases.

A sign of the economic depression in Germany. In Berlin, hundreds of cars are stored in a garage to avoid heavy taxation.

AMERICA'S ECONOMIC CRISIS

Dec 11, Washington   America's economic problems are getting worse. A major bank, the Bank of the United States, has collapsed. Half a million people kept their savings there. Now it has no money to pay them and they have lost everything.

ECONOMIC CRISIS IS WORLDWIDE

Dec,   It has been estimated that 30 million people are without work in the industrial countries of the world. No nation has escaped the crisis. The position in Germany is particularly bad. Nearly half of all men between 16 and 30 are without jobs.

GANDHI DEFIES BRITISH LAWS

May 4, Dandi, India The British authorities have arrested Mahatma Gandhi. His crime was picking up and eating a piece of salt! In India, salt is taxed and only the Government is allowed to make and sell it. Gandhi came to Dandi on foot with a few followers. He walked down to the sea, picked up some dried salt from the sand, and ate it. By doing that, he broke the law. Thousands of Indians have now done the same. The British cannot arrest them all, so they have arrested Gandhi.

The Mahatma plans to go on breaking British laws, but never to use violence. Millions of Indians obey Gandhi and if they follow his example, British rule will break down and India will win independence.

Gandhi (marked by an arrow) and some followers defying the law by picking up salt.

Nazis triumph in German elections

Sept 15, Berlin The National Socialist Party has won 107 seats in the German parliament. It is now the second largest party in Germany behind the Socialists. The National Socialists have shortened their name to 'Nazi'. Their leader is Herr Adolf Hitler. Some people say that he will become Chancellor of Germany before long.

THE TERRIBLE PENALTY OF BEING RICH IN RUSSIA

March, Moscow The richer peasants in Russia have suffered a terrible fate in the recent changes. These peasants, or 'kulaks' as they are called, have not been allowed to join the new collective farms. On Stalin's orders, the men are sent to concentration camps. The women and children have been packed off to Siberia, without proper food or shelter. As a result about a million families have been condemned to die from overwork, cold or starvation.

Millions of Russian peasants forced to move

Feb, Moscow The Soviet government claims that half the peasants in Russia have joined collective farms. Russia is a huge country. Most of its people work on the land. The government statement means that no fewer than 60 million people have been forced to move from their homes inside two months. These changes have been forced on the Russian people by their leader, Josef Stalin.

Russian peasants recovering hidden grain that would otherwise be taken by the government.

NEWS IN BRIEF . . .

NEW PLANET DISCOVERED

March 18, Arizona, USA An astronomer working at the Lovell Observatory has discovered a new planet going round the sun. He has called it Pluto, after the Greek God of the Underworld.

AMY JOHNSON'S HISTORIC FLIGHT

April 24, Darwin, Australia An old Gipsy Moth aeroplane landed here this evening. Its pilot, Miss Amy Johnson, has become the first woman to fly solo from Britain to Australia.

Miss Johnson is a very brave woman. She had only 100 hours' flying experience before making the journey to Australia in her second-hand aeroplane. She brought a bag of tools with her and serviced the plane herself at every stop along the way. When it landed, parts of it were patched up with sticking plaster!

The *Daily Mail* is to give Miss Johnson a prize of £10,000 for making her historic flight.

The skeleton of the *R101* airship which crashed on its maiden flight.

THE WORLD'S LARGEST AIRSHIP IS DESTROYED

Oct 5, Beauvais, France The British airship *R101* crashed here early this morning and burst into flames. It flew into a hillside and exploded. Only 8 people survived of the 54 on board.

NAZIS ATTACK JEWS IN GERMANY

Oct 15, Berlin The Nazi leader, Herr Adolf Hitler has made many threats against the Jews. His followers are now carrying them out. Crowds of Nazi supporters have paraded through the streets of Berlin shouting 'Death to the Jews!' Nazi party members dressed in their brownshirt uniforms have broken Jewish shop windows and smashed up what is inside. There are reports that the Nazis have also attacked Jews in other parts of Germany.

HAILE SELASSIE CROWNED EMPEROR OF ABYSSINIA

Nov 2, Addis Ababa, Abyssinia Thousands of warriors dressed in lion-skin cloaks have come to Addis Ababa to see their Emperor crowned. There are only two black rulers in the whole of Africa. Emperor Haile Selassie is one. The President of Liberia is the other.

1931

HUGE SPENDING CUTS PROPOSED

July 31, London A committee set up by the Labour government has advised huge cuts in public spending. The proposals tell the government to reduce the pay of teachers, the police and the armed forces and to lower payments to the unemployed.

These proposed measures show how badly Britain has been hit by the world economic crisis. They also suggest that the present government is not able to solve the problems that face Britain today.

National Government formed

Aug 24, London The Labour government has fallen. It could not carry on because several of its members resigned. They refused to accept the proposals made by the Economy Committee to cut wages and unemployment pay.

A new government has been formed. Members of all the main political parties are to join and it will be called a 'National Government'. The present Prime Minister, Mr Ramsay Macdonald (seated, centre below) is staying on as leader.

Serious outbreak of fighting in Manchuria

Sept 19, Manchuria, Northern China Fighting has broken out between Japanese and Chinese troops. The Japanese have captured the Chinese city of Mukden. They blame China for starting the trouble. The Japanese authorities say that they drove Chinese troops out of Mukden to stop them blowing up the railway line that runs through the city. The Chinese deny this.

The Japanese hold southern Manchuria on lease from China. They have factories and mines in the area, and they own the railway. Troops from Japan are stationed there to protect Japan's interests. The fighting continues.

Japan's economy has been badly hit by the current Depression. The attack on Mukden, in Manchuria, is seen as the first step in a policy of expansion into China which would provide a vast market for Japanese goods.

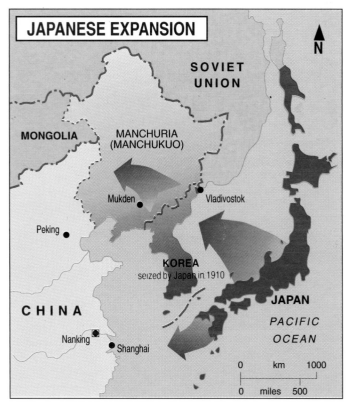

JAPANESE EXPANSION

SOVIET UNION

MONGOLIA

MANCHURIA (MANCHUKUO)

Mukden

Vladivostok

Peking

KOREA
seized by Japan in 1910

CHINA

JAPAN

PACIFIC OCEAN

Nanking

Shanghai

0 km 1000

0 miles 500

Manchurian conquest strengthens war party in Japan

Dec 30, Tokyo, Japan Japanese troops have driven the Chinese from Manchuria. A warlike spirit has seized Japan and it is not safe to speak out against it. The government is despised for giving in to the League of Nations. Power is falling into the hands of those who wish Japan to conquer an empire.

SPAIN BECOMES A REPUBLIC

April 14, Madrid, Spain The socialists have won the elections. King Alfonso has gone into exile and Spain will now become a republic. Church and army leaders are bitterly opposed to this prospect. They fear a republic would be the first step towards communism. They would fight to prevent it.

SAILORS STRIKE OVER PAY

Sept 18, Britain Three days ago, British sailors at Invergordon went on strike over cuts in their pay. They have gone back to duty today, but their protest has caused great alarm. The Government made the pay cuts to try to save money. This strike is another example of the trouble caused by the bad state of Britain's economy.

SLAVE LABOUR IN RUSSIA

Oct 1, Moscow Russians who oppose their leader Stalin face a grim future. They are shut up in prison camps and made to work like slaves. Hundreds of thousands of these slave workers are toiling day and night, in all weathers, to build a canal that will link the Baltic Sea with the White Sea off Russia's northern coast. When finished the canal will be 227km long. The Russians plan to complete it in two years.

NEWS IN BRIEF . . .

HUGE EARTHQUAKE IN NEW ZEALAND

Feb 3, New Zealand A violent earthquake has almost destroyed the towns of Napier and Hastings in New Zealand's North Island. Over two hundred people died as their houses collapsed upon them – 950 have been injured and 10,000 are homeless.

MALCOLM CAMPBELL SETS NEW RECORD

Feb 5, Daytona Beach, Florida, USA Captain Campbell today raised his own world landspeed record. In his streamlined *Blue Bird* motor car he set a new time of 245mph.

Captain Campbell in his *Blue Bird*. The car is designed with an unusual tail-plane, suggesting an aeroplane body on wheels.

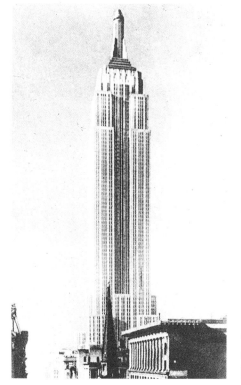

THE WORLD'S TALLEST BUILDING OPENED

May 1, New York President Hoover has opened the world's tallest building here in New York. He named it the Empire State Building. It has 86 floors and is 381m high (1238 feet). It contains 10,000,000 bricks, and there is an airship mooring-mast at the top.

The Empire State Building which was opened by President Hoover in New York.

A NATION OF FILM-GOERS

Sept, London The cinema has become the most popular form of entertainment in Britain. A recent survey reveals that over 40 per cent of British people visit a cinema at least once every week.

'SCARFACE' AL CAPONE GOES TO JAIL

Oct 22, USA 'Scarface' Al Capone, the gangster who made millions from selling illegal alcohol, has been jailed for 11 years. No one was brave enough to give evidence against Capone. The FBI got him in the end for not paying his taxes!

DEATH OF THOMAS EDISON

Oct 18, New Jersey, USA Thomas Alva Edison died here today aged 84. Edison made over a thousand inventions. He invented the electric light bulb, the phonograph (or gramophone) and many of the devices that make cinema films possible. Edison will be buried on October 21. Lights across America will be dimmed for one minute that day, in his honour.

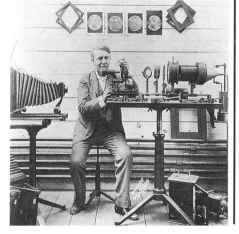

1932

CHINESE GOVERNMENT BANS JAPANESE GOODS

Jan 4, Nanking, China The Chinese government has placed a ban on all imports from Japan. Officials say the ban will stay until the Japanese end the fighting in Manchuria. The ban will hurt the Japanese badly. They depend on the huge Chinese market for the sale of their goods.

WAR SPREADS TO CHINA

Feb 4, Shanghai, China The ban on Japanese goods has not stopped the war in Manchuria. The fighting has spread to China itself. A few days ago, the Japanese army in Manchuria launched a successful attack on Shanghai, China's greatest port. The Japanese claim they have seized Shanghai to punish the Chinese for banning their goods.

One of the Chinese trenches in Shanghai.

MANCHURIA BECOMES MANCHUKUO

Feb 19, Manchukuo Japan now controls Manchuria, and has re-named the country Manchukuo. The Japanese claim that Manchukuo is a free and independent state. In fact, the new government takes its orders from the Japanese authorities in Tokyo. The truth is that Manchukuo is now part of the Japanese empire.

JAPAN'S PRIME MINISTER KILLED

March 16, Tokyo Prime Minister Inukai of Japan has been murdered. Last night, a group of young officers entered his house and shot him dead. Inukai angered the army when he tried to end the war in Manchuria. This is why he was killed. His murderers belong to the 'League of Blood', a secret society of officers that aims to make Japan great by conquering an empire. Japan is now in ther hands. The prospects for peace are bleak.

Prime Minister Inukai of Japan.

15

America's new young President

Nov 8, Washington Americans have elected a new leader. Out goes President Hoover. In comes Franklin D. Roosevelt.

Mr. Roosevelt is 38 years old, and has been a successful and popular Governor of New York State. He is paralysed from the waist down by polio but his handicap has not reduced his energy, or his cheerfulness. The hopes of America will be with this young politician when he takes over as President next year.

America's new President, Franklin D. Roosevelt seen campaigning for votes in Pittsburgh. The main issue in the election was the trade depression and unemployment.

GANDHI ARRESTED BY BRITISH

Jan 6, Delhi, India Two days ago, Mahatma Gandhi was arrested by the British authorities. Today other leading members of the Indian National Congress Party are being rounded up and imprisoned.

The British, who rule India, have promised that one day India will have self-government. Gandhi and his followers want independence now. Their Congress Party has been declared illegal.

Herr Hitler loses the election, but claims a victory

April 10, Berlin Field Marshal von Hindenburg remains President of Germany. In the election he beat Adolf Hitler, leader of the Nazi party, by six million votes.

Although Hitler did not win the election he easily came second. The Nazis received over three times more votes than their chief enemies, the Communists. Herr Hitler claims this as a great victory.

HUGE INCREASE IN THE NAZI VOTE IN GERMANY

July 31, Berlin The Nazi party has more than doubled the number of seats it holds in the German Parliament. They are now the largest party in the Reichstag. However, they cannot form a government to rule the country because they have fewer seats than the other parties combined.

HUNGER MARCHERS IN LONDON

Oct 27, "The workers kept the police back from the meetings; several times mounted police charged forward, only to be repulsed by thousands of workers who tore up railings and used them as weapons and barricades for the protection of their meetings. Many mounted men were dragged from their horses. From the streets the fighting extended into the park and back again into the streets, where repeated mounted police charges at full speed failed to dislodge the workers. The foot police were on several occasions surrounded by strong forces of workers, and terrific fights ensued."

(Wal Hannington, *Unemployed Struggles 1919–36*, © 1936 Lawrence and Wishart Ltd, London)

NEWS IN BRIEF . . .

MAN WHO MADE PHOTOGRAPHY EASY DIES

March 14, Rochester, USA George Eastman made taking photographs easy and cheap. Over 50 years ago he invented roll film, and a camera to use it in. He called his camera a 'Kodak'. He thought up this phrase to sell it: "You press the button, we do the rest". The Kodak sold in millions, and George Eastman became a very rich man. He was generous, too. In 1930, he gave away half a million of his cameras to the children of the USA. George Eastman died today. He was 77.

George Eastman pictured with his Kodak camera.

SYDNEY'S NEW BRIDGE

May 19, Sydney, Australia The new bridge over Sydney's magnificent harbour was opened today. It is 503m long and 48m wide, and is the largest bridge of its kind in the world. It carries eight lanes for cars, a cycleway, two railway tracks as well as pavements for people on foot.

AMERICA'S AMELIA EARHART SETS ATLANTIC RECORD

May 21, Dublin, Ireland Amelia Earhart is the first woman to fly the Atlantic alone. She also made the journey in record time. Her solo flight from Newfoundland to Western Ireland took 15 hours and 18 minutes.

THE LOS ANGELES OLYMPIC GAMES

Aug 14, Los Angeles The USA has won more medals than any other country at the Los Angeles Games. Few competitors came from Europe. The journey by ship and train costs too much and takes too long. For the first time in any Games, the men athletes lived in an 'Olympic Village' built specially for the occasion. The women stayed in hotels. There were other 'firsts' in these Games. Electrical devices timed the track events and the races were filmed by movie cameras.

WINNING LAND FROM THE SEA IN HOLLAND

Aug, The Hague, Holland Dutch engineers are busy building walls around shallow stretches of sea along the Dutch coast. When the wall is finished, the sea water inside is pumped out. After the sea bed has dried out it becomes rich farmland. The engineers have finished a wall 32km long around part of the Zuider Zee. The Dutch say their drainage plans will make Holland 6 per cent larger than it is today.

A FRIGHTENING VIEW OF THE FUTURE

Sept, London The most talked-about novel of the year is Aldous Huxley's *Brave New World*. The story is set in Britain many years in the future. Babies are mass-produced in test-tubes in a factory. Drugs keep the people contented and obedient. Not all the things Mr Huxley writes about are impossible. Some of them could happen now!

1933

GERMANY'S NEW LEADER
ADOLF HITLER TO LEAD GERMANY

Jan 30, Berlin President von Hindenburg has appointed the Nazi leader Adolf Hitler Chancellor of Germany. Herr Hitler names Jews and Communists Germany's chief enemies and has boasted that he will destroy them. Now that he has the power, many fear he will do so.

The first picture of Herr Adolf Hitler (centre) and his ministers after his appointment as Chancellor of Germany.

FIRE WRECKS REICHSTAG

Feb 28, Last night the Reichstag building in Berlin, home of Germany's parliament, was set alight. The fire was watched by Germany's new Chancellor, Herr Hitler, who had hurried to the scene. A young Dutchman said to have been found in the building has been held for questioning by the police. He is believed to be a Communist.

As a result German police across the country are rounding up leading Communists and others known to oppose the Nazi party.

HITLER ACCUSES THE COMMUNISTS

March 1, Chancellor Hitler has issued a proclamation blaming the Communists for the Reichstag fire. He warns the German people that the blaze was meant as a signal for a Communist revolution to break out. Swift action by the police, acting on his orders, put the criminals behind bars, he claims.

Hitler voted dictator of Germany

March 23, Nazi members cheered wildly as Germany's parliament gave Chancellor Hitler the power to make his own laws. The vote was a farce, for nearly all members of parliament who would have voted against Hitler have been arrested, or are in hiding. But under the new Act, Hitler becomes legally the absolute, unchallenged ruler of Germany.

THE REICHSTAG FIRE

Feb 27, "The fire broke out at 9.45 tonight in the Assembly Hall of the Reichstag. . . Five minutes after the fire had broken out I was outside the Reichstag watching the flames licking their way up the great dome into the tower.

After about twenty minutes of fascinated watching I suddenly saw the famous black motor car of Adolf Hitler slide past, followed by another car containing his personal bodyguard. I rushed after them and was just in time to attach myself to the fringe of Hitler's party as they entered the Reichstag.

We strode across a lobby filled with smoke. The police barred the way. 'The candelabra may crash any moment, Herr Chancellor,' said a captain of the police, with his arms outstretched. By a detour we next reached a part of the building which was actually in flames. Firemen were pouring water into the red mass. Hitler watched them for a few moments, a savage fury blazing from his pale blue eyes. . .

It was then that Hitler turned to me. 'God grant,' he said, 'that this is the work of the Communists. You are witnessing the beginning of a great new epoch in German history. This fire is the beginning.' "

(D. Sefton Delmer,
Daily Express, 28 Feb 1933)

The ruins of the Reichstag.

Spain in turmoil

Jan 20, Madrid Disorder is spreading throughout Spain. Rival right and left wing groups of peasants and workers are in violent conflict. Parliament has given Prime Minister Azaña power to use troops to keep order, but parts of the country are already controlled by the military. Spain seems to be heading for civil war.

CONCENTRATION CAMPS

March 20, Berlin Germany's Nazi Government is determined to crush all resistance. Establishments called 'concentration camps' are planned as places where those who oppose Nazi rule will be held for what is termed 're-education and training'. The first of these camps has opened at Dachau near Munich. The job of running it has been given to Munich's police chief, Heinrich Himmler.

WALKOUTS WEAKEN THE LEAGUE

Oct 14, Geneva Germany has joined Japan and walked out of the League of Nations. In Berlin, Herr Hitler blames unjust and insulting treatment of his country for the withdrawal.

These walkouts have seriously weakened the League's authority. Few now believe that it has the power to keep the world at peace.

New US President's words of hope

March 4, Washington Franklin Delano Roosevelt has been sworn in as President of the United States. In his election address he promised a 'New Deal' for America. Now in a stirring first speech as President, he has outlined 100 days of action to set America on the road to recovery. "The only thing we have to fear, is fear itself," is his brave message to the American people.

NEWS IN BRIEF . . .

"WAR IN 7 YEARS" SAYS H. G. WELLS

A second world war breaking out in 1940 is the frightening theme of H. G. Wells' latest scientific romance *The Shape of Things to Come*. This story of the future describes the world in ruins after nine years of world conflict. But a world government is set up after the war, and all the people of the Earth live happily together in peace and justice.

THE LATEST FASHIONS FOR WOMEN!

THE WORLD'S FINEST CAR

Latest in the line of superb motor cars produced by the Rolls-Royce company is the 40–50 hp Phantom II. With a continental body and weighing 2½ tons, it can reach a top speed of over 90 mph. Fuel consumption ranges from 10 mpg in town, to 14 mpg on the open road. Price, with a continental touring body, is £2425.

BAD TABLE MANNERS WIN OSCAR!

In the banquet scene from the British film *The Private Life of Henry VIII*, the beefy monarch rips meat with his bare fingers, and tosses half-eaten legs of chicken over his shoulder! British actor Charles Laughton plays the king and clearly enjoys this display of bad table manners. Charles Laughton's performance has won him an Oscar as cinema's best actor for 1933.

LONDON FILMS PROUDLY PRESENT CHARLES LAUGHTON IN "THE PRIVATE LIFE of HENRY VIII"

NEW LANDSPEED RECORD

March 22, Driving his *Blue Bird* motor car at Daytona Beach, Florida, Britain's Sir Malcolm Campbell has set a new world landspeed record at 272 mph.

FIRST SOLO FLIGHT AROUND THE WORLD

May 22, American pilot Wiley Post has become the first person to make a solo flight around the world. Flying a Lockheed Vega aircraft called *Winnie Mae*, the journey took 7 days, 18 hours, 49 minutes.

ALCOHOLIC DRINK ON SALE AGAIN IN USA

Dec 31, On December 5 the law banning alcoholic drink in the United States was ended. Soon it will be possible to buy alcohol, legally, anywhere in the country.

The ban was called 'Prohibition'. It led to war between rival criminal gangs who fought over the huge fortunes made from selling illegal liquor.

1934

July 19   British Royal Air Force to be increased
July 25   Austrian Chancellor murdered
Oct   Chinese Red Army on the march
Dec   Border fighting in Abyssinia

LEADING NAZIS KILLED

June 30, Munich The leading Nazi Ernst Roehm has been murdered. Several of his closest friends died with him. They were staying at a luxury hotel near Munich. There are strong rumours that hundreds of other members of the Nazi party have been killed elsewhere in Germany.

DOUBTS CAST ON HITLER'S STORY

July 26, Vienna, Austria More information has been given about the murder of the Austrian Chancellor. After the Nazi gunmen were surrounded they tried to bargain for a safe passage to the German border. If they knew that they would be safe in Germany, it casts doubt on Hitler's word that Germany had nothing to do with the crime.

Adolf Hitler at a Nazi Party rally with some of his supporters. It is believed that Hitler himself ordered the murder of hundreds of Nazi Storm Troopers. This group had helped Hitler's rise to power by disposing of his opponents.

THE AUSTRIAN CHANCELLOR MURDERED

July 25, Vienna, Austria At noon today, armed men entered the offices of Herr Dollfuss, Chancellor of Austria. They made straight for the Chancellor and shot him at point blank range. Police and troops swiftly surrounded the building, but they were unable to save Herr Dollfuss. The gunmen would not let a doctor in to see him, and he bled to death. It has been revealed that Herr Dollfuss was shot by members of the Austrian Nazi Party. They are to be put on trial for murder.

Herr Hitler spoke about the tragic events earlier today in Vienna. He said there are no links between the German Nazi Party and the Austrian Nazis who shot Herr Dollfuss.

Austrian Chancellor Dr Dollfuss lies in state guarded by soldiers of the federal army.

THE STRUGGLE FOR CHINA

March, Kiangsi Province, China The Communists occupy part of Kiangsi Province in southern China. They are led by a man who was once a peasant. His name is Mao Tse-Tung. He calls his followers 'The Red Army'. Mao and the Communists are fighting General Chiang Kai-Shek and his Nationalist army for the control of China.

Mao's Red Army is in great danger. General Chiang Kai-Shek's forces have surrounded it with a ring of concrete blockhouses and barbed-wire fences. General Chiang intends to starve the Red Army into surrender by cutting off its supplies.

THE RED ARMY BREAKS OUT

Oct, Kiangsi Province, China The Red Army is on the move. It has broken through Chiang Kai-Shek's troops and is travelling westward toward Kweichow. Mao is keeping away from towns and cities, and is leading his troops through areas where there are very few people. The Nationalists are attacking them along the way, but so far have failed to stop the march of Mao's men.

HITLER THE SPEECH-MAKER

Herr Hitler prepares his speeches as carefully as an actor preparing for a play. First, he makes a recording of what he is going to say. Then he listens to it, over and over again, and practises the gestures and the movements he will use when he delivers the speech to an audience. Huge crowds are hypnotised by his performance. The power of his speech-making helps to explain why the German people are so willing to follow him.

Hitler has promised to build a new Germany, where the people would have jobs and new pride in their country. He is known for his emotional and often violent speeches made before vast numbers of supporters at Nazi Party rallies.

Britain's Royal Air Force to be increased

July 19, London MPs cheered today when Prime Minister Baldwin announced in the House of Commons that 41 new squadrons are to be added to Britain's air defences by 1938. The news pleased most MPs, but some fear that the RAF is still smaller than other airforces in Europe.

Italy in border shooting

Dec 18, Abyssinian border Shots have been fired across the border between Abyssinian and Italian troops in East Africa. Each side blames the other for firing first. Since the shooting, Italian planes have bombed two Abyssinian villages near the frontier.

NEWS IN BRIEF . . .

GERMAN CHILDREN READY TO DIE FOR HITLER

Germany When they are ten, boys in Germany have to join the Young Peoples' Movement. They wear miniature Nazi uniforms and are drilled like soldiers. When they join the movement they go through a special ceremony. They stand under a Nazi flag and say this:

"Under this flag, I swear to give all my strength to Adolf Hitler, the man who saved our country. I am willing and ready to die for him, so help me God."

COMPOSER SIR EDWARD ELGAR DIES

Feb 23, Worcester, England Sir Edward Elgar died today, aged 76. His symphonies, concertos and choral works have become famous worldwide. He is perhaps best known for composing *Land of Hope and Glory*, which is sometimes called England's second national anthem.

THE GERMAN GREETING

Germany People in Germany are greeting one another in a new way. When two people meet, they thrust out their right arms straight toward each other and say 'Heil Hitler!'

The Nazi government has ordered all Germans to use this form of greeting in future.

SHORTS AT WIMBLEDON

May, London Women competitors are to be allowed to wear shorts instead of skirts at this year's Wimbledon tennis championships. The decision has upset many male officials. They argue that those who play at Wimbledon should set an example of how to dress properly. They say that shorts are vulgar and unfeminine for women.

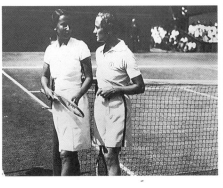

DEATH OF MARIE CURIE

July 4, France Marie Curie, the world's greatest woman scientist, has died aged 66. Madame Curie was born in Poland, but came to France to study science. She married the French scientist Pierre Curie, and in 1903 they were jointly awarded a Nobel Prize for their discovery of radium and radioactivity. Marie Curie died of a blood disease caused by working with radioactive materials.

DILLINGER DEAD

July 22, Chicago, USA John Dillinger, bank robber and murderer of 16 people, lies dead this evening outside a Chicago cinema. The police were taking no chances with the man who has outwitted them several times before. Dillinger fell under a storm of police bullets as he came out into the street. He had been watching a gangster film!

NEW OCEAN LINER LAUNCHED

Sept 26, Glasgow, Scotland The first ship in history to weigh over 75,000 tonnes was launched at the John Brown shipyards today. The monster ocean liner will join the Cunard White Star fleet on the Atlantic run, between Southampton and New York. It is expected to go into service in 1936. The new ship's name will be *Queen Mary*.

1935

HITLER TEARS UP THE VERSAILLES TREATY

March 16, Berlin Hitler has scrapped the treaty that ended World War I. The treaty limited the size of Germany's army and navy, and banned her from having an air force. Hitler's move enables him to build up Germany's armed forces exactly as he pleases. He has already announced that all young men in Germany will receive military training.

Train-loads of cheering troops are leaving Rome to swell the ever-growing Italian army in East Africa.

RISK OF WAR IN EAST AFRICA

May, Since February, thousands of Italian troops have been moved to the frontier between Italian East Africa and Abyssinia. Signor Mussolini blames Abyssinia. He claims that Abyssinian soldiers have fired across the border, and that Italian troops have been sent to stop them. The Abyssinians deny it. They say that the Italians are inventing reasons for invading their country. They have asked the League of Nations for protection.

A group of Abyssinian soldiers on the march – without shoes!

ITALY INVADES ABYSSINIA

Oct 3, Italian East Africa Thousands of Italian troops crossed the border into Abyssinia at dawn this morning. The Italians have the most modern weapons, including at least 200 tanks. The Abyssinians are armed with simple rifles, and many have only spears and bows and arrows to fight with.

BRITAIN JOINS THE ARMS RACE

May 22, London Britain has joined the rest of Europe in building up her armed forces. Earlier this year, the government revealed plans to increase spending on defence. Today, Prime Minister Stanley Baldwin announced that Britain's Royal Air Force is to get 1500 new aircraft. This new strength will make the RAF as big as the airforce Hitler has ordered for Germany.

NO GUNS FOR ITALY

Nov 18, Geneva The League of Nations is at last trying to force Mussolini to end his invasion of Abyssinia. Fifty countries have agreed not to sell war weapons or supplies to Italy. However, the ban is likely to fail since oil is not included. So long as Italy can buy oil for her armed forces and her industries, Mussolini will be able to continue the war against Abyssinia.

STALIN'S IRON GRIP ON RUSSIA

March 9, Moscow Stalin is filling all key posts in the Soviet Union with his supporters. The latest to benefit is Nikita Khrushchev. He is appointed head of the Communist Party in the capital, Moscow.

Punishment of all who oppose Stalin goes on. Even his closest friends have suffered. Some have been murdered. Others rot away in prison. Their only crime was to oppose the leader, Stalin.

MAO'S LONG MARCH

Oct 20, Shensi Province, China The Red Army has reached northern China. In this remote place it will be safe from attack by Chiang Kai-Shek's Nationalist forces. The Red Army has travelled over 9000 km in the year since it broke out of its base in the south. Only 30,000 soldiers remain of the 100,000 that set out. 'The Long March' as Mao calls it, is the longest march in the history of war.

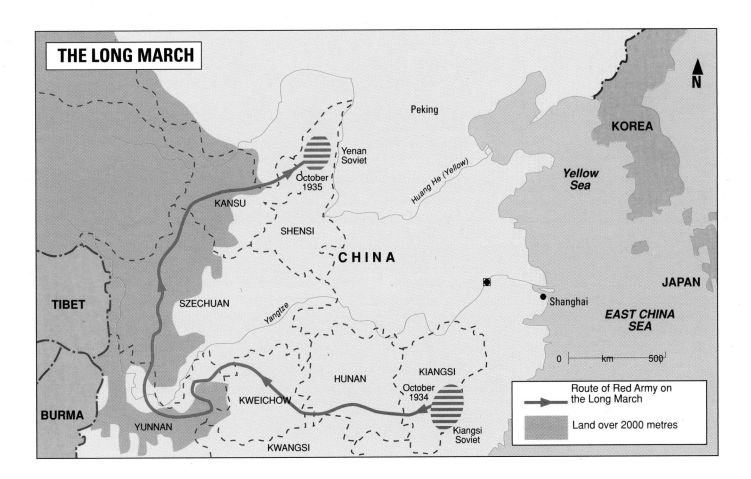

THE LONG MARCH

Route of Red Army on the Long March

Land over 2000 metres

NEWS IN BRIEF . . .

DUST DEVASTATES THE HEART OF AMERICA

April 15, USA   Blinding dust storms have destroyed the rich farming country in America's heartland. The choking dust clouds have ruined crops worth millions of dollars and driven thousands from their homes.

GOOD BOOKS EVERYONE CAN AFFORD

July, London   Penguins are in the shops! 'Penguin' is the name of a new family of books published by Mr Allen Lane. The books are paperbacks and cost only sixpence (2½p) each.

Penguins are not trashy rubbish, like most other paperbacks. They are books written by famous authors, and sold at a price which people can afford.

NAZIS BAN JAZZ MUSIC

Oct, Berlin   The Nazis have banned all jazz music composed by Jews and Negroes from German radio. The official announcement claims that such music is poor quality and that it will do young Germans no good to listen to it.

NEW ALTITUDE RECORD

Nov 11, USA   Two Americans have set a new altitude record for balloons. They reached a height of 22,500 metres (15,000 miles).

MALCOLM CAMPBELL'S NEW WORLD RECORD

Sept 3, Bonneville Salt Flats, Utah, USA   Sir Malcolm Campbell has broken the world landspeed record for the **eighth** time! He has taken his monster car *Bluebird* across the bed of this dried-up lake near Salt Lake City at 301 mph.

Sir Malcolm says that this is his last high speed drive on land. He now means to go for the world speed record on water!

GERSHWIN'S *PORGY AND BESS* OPENS

Sept 30, Boston, Massachusetts   An all-black cast perform George Gershwin's opera *Porgy and Bess* which opens in Boston today. Critics predict it will become an American classic. The song *Summertime* is likely to become an all-time favourite.

1936

Jan 20   Britain has a new King
May 9   Italy conquers Abyssinia
July 31   Civil war in Spain
Dec 10   King Edward VIII abdicates
Dec 12   George VI is new British King

BRITAIN'S NEW KING

Jan 20, London King George V has died, aged 70. He reigned for 25 years and celebrated his Silver Jubilee only last year.

The King's eldest son Edward, Prince of Wales, now succeeds to the throne. He will take the title of King Edward VIII. The new King is unmarried. Until he marries and has children, the heir to the throne is his younger brother, the Duke of York.

A KING IN LOVE

Dec 3, London Newspapers in Britain have at last printed the news that the King wishes to marry Mrs Wallis Simpson. Newspapers in Europe and America have been full of the King's love affair for months. Mrs Simpson is an American and has been married twice before.

King Edward gives up the throne

Dec 10, London King Edward VIII has abdicated. He has given up the throne. His brother, the Duke of York, is now King.

Political and religious leaders in Britain and the British Commonwealth tried to persuade King Edward to give up Mrs Simpson. They told him that his people would not accept a woman who had been married before, as their queen. But Edward would not change his mind. He has chosen to give up the throne in order to marry Mrs Simpson.

ROOSEVELT WINS AGAIN

Nov 3, Washington The American people have elected Franklin D. Roosevelt to be their President for the second time. He won by the largest margin of votes in American history.

Most Americans are grateful to their President. His 'New Deal' policy has given them jobs, and saved their homes, their farms and their savings.

THE NEW ROYAL FAMILY

Dec 12, London The ex-King Edward VIII has left the country. His brother, the new King George VI, has created him Duke of Windsor.

King George and his wife Queen Elizabeth have two daughters. The elder, Princess Elizabeth, is ten years old. She becomes heir to the throne of Britain, the Commonwealth and the Empire.

CIVIL WAR IN SPAIN

SPANISH CIVIL WAR (July/August 1936)

Legend:
- Initial advance of Nationalists
- Nationalist territory
- Republican territory

July 31, Spain The Spanish army has rebelled against the Government. General Franco, the army's leader, has accused the Government of turning Spain into a communist state. He has founded a new political party, the Nationalists, to oppose communism and has appealed to all Spaniards to join it.

Spaniards who side with the Government call themselves 'Republicans'. They out number Franco's supporters, but Franco controls the army. In reply, the Republicans have formed an army of their own. Compared with Franco's forces, they are poorly trained and short of weapons. Fighting between the two sides is going on in many places. Spain is in the grip of civil war.

'VOLUNTEERS' FIGHT IN SPAIN

Dec 31, Madrid There is no end in sight to the fighting in Spain. The war has spread. Italian and German troops and aircraft are serving with Franco's Nationalist forces. Russia is backing the Republicans with money, troops and equipment. But the governments of these countries deny that they are involved in the war. They claim that all their men fighting in Spain are volunteers.

ITALY CONQUERS ABYSSINIA

May 9, Italian troops have occupied Addis Ababa, the capital of Abyssinia. The Emperor and most of his family have escaped abroad. It is believed that he will make his home in Britain. The city of Rome has gone wild. Signor Benito Mussolini, speaking from a balcony to huge cheering crowds below, has proclaimed that Abyssinia belongs to Italy. "At last Italy has her empire," he said.

An Italian military governor will rule the new possession and the King of Italy will take the title 'Emperor of Abyssinia'.

German troops enter the Rhineland

March 6, French/German border Hitler's troops have occupied the Rhineland. After World War I, this strip of land between Germany and France was made neutral. No troops were to be stationed there. The area was meant to be a buffer between the two countries to keep them apart.

Other European powers have protested to Germany for taking over the Rhineland, but it is unlikely that they will try to force her to withdraw. They are frightened of Germany's growing strength, and are terrified of starting another war.

A street patrol in Barcelona. Civilians armed by the government use an old horse-drawn wagon for patrol duties.

NEWS IN BRIEF . . .

A NEW CAR FOR GERMANY

Feb 26, Wolfsburg, Germany The Germans mean to become a nation on wheels – like the Americans! Herr Hitler has opened a new factory here, to produce a cheap, reliable car which every family will be able to afford. It is called 'The People's Car'. Its German name is *Volkswagen*.

RECORD ATLANTIC CROSSING

July, New Jersey, USA The giant German airship *Hindenburg* has crossed the Atlantic in under two days. If the present tests continue to go well Germany will start a regular service across the Atlantic next year.

JESSE OWENS TRIUMPHS

Aug 15, Berlin The XIth Olympic Games ended today. Germany and the USA have won most medals. The outstanding athlete of the Games is the black American runner Jesse Owens. He won four gold medals.

This triumph has enraged Germany's Nazi rulers. They claim that black people are inferior to whites. Yet, at the Berlin Games, a black athlete has shown he is the best in the world.

KING EDWARD'S FAREWELL SPEECH

Dec 11, London Edward VIII made a farewell speech to his people by radio this evening. This is part of what he said:

"At long last, I am able to say a few words of my own . . . I want you to understand that in making up my mind I did not forget the country or the Empire which as Prince of Wales and lately as King, I have for 25 years tried to serve. But you must believe me when I tell you that I have found it impossible to carry the heavy burden of responsibility and to discharge my duties as King as I would wish to do without the help and support of the woman I love . . . God bless you all. God save the King."

A 'NEW' CHRISTMAS CAROL

Dec 14, London Children in Britain are singing a new song. It goes to the tune of a well-known Christmas carol. Here it is:

"Hark the herald angels sing
Mrs Simpson's pinched our King."

1937

THE INTERNATIONAL BRIGADES

Feb 20, Spain Volunteers from many countries are coming to Spain to take part in the war. Nearly all have joined the Republican side to fight General Franco. Many have had to come in secret. In some countries, like Britain, it is against the law to go to Spain to fight. The volunteers go into battle in units called the 'International Brigades'.

GUERNICA DESTROYED

April 26, Spanish civil war ". . . I was the first correspondent to reach Guernica, and was immediately pressed into service by some Basque soldiers. . . .

In the Plaza, surrounded almost by a wall of fire, were about a hundred refugees. They were wailing and weeping and rocking to and fro. One middle-aged man spoke English. He told me, 'At four, before the market closed, many aeroplanes came. They dropped bombs. Some came low and shot bullets into the streets. . . .'

The man had no idea who I was, as far as I knew. He was telling me what had happened to Guernica. . . . I moved round to the back of the Plaza among the survivors. They had the same story to tell, aeroplanes, bullets, bombs, fire."

(Noel Monks, *Eye witness*, Frederick Muller 1955)

THE BOMBING OF GUERNICA

April 30, Northern Spain Guernica has been destroyed. More than 100 aircraft from the German Condor Legion dropped tons of fire and high-explosive bombs on this defenceless small city. It was market day and the streets were crowded. The bombers came without warning. Over 2000 men, women and children were killed or injured.

The bombing of Guernica has aroused shock and anger throughout the world. Newspapers in Spain that support General Franco blame the other side. They claim that Republican troops deliberately destroyed Guernica before leaving it. Their story is a lie. From all reports and from the people who were there, it is certain that German bombers destroyed Guernica.

FRANCO IS WINNING THE WAR

Oct 21, Northern Spain General Franco's forces are winning the civil war in Spain. Today they have captured the town of Gijon and 6000 Republican prisoners. The Nationalists now control most of the country.

JAPANESE TAKE PEKING

July 28, Peking China After three weeks of heavy fighting the Japanese have taken the city of Peking. More Japanese troops are pouring into China and are making for the port of Tientsin. They are likely to capture it in the next few days.

SHANGHAI FALLS TO THE JAPANESE

Nov 9, Shanghai After three months of savage fighting, the Japanese have captured Shanghai. The loss of Shanghai, their greatest port, is a great blow to the Chinese.

The League of Nations has condemned the Japanese attack on China, but the Japanese have taken no notice. The Chinese have appealed for help to the League but no country is prepared to go to their aid. Once more, it seems the League is powerless to keep peace in the world.

Buildings blazing in Shanghai after a Japanese air bomb set the city alight.

GEORGE VI CROWNED KING

May 12, London King George and Queen Elizabeth were crowned this morning in Westminster Abbey.

The King and Queen's two daughters, Princess Elizabeth and Princess Margaret, aged eleven and six-and-a-half, watched the ceremony. Afterwards, the royal family returned to their home at Buckingham Palace and stood on the balcony to wave to the huge crowd waiting below.

Chamberlain becomes British Prime Minister

May 28, London Neville Chamberlain has become Prime Minister. He succeeds Stanley Baldwin, who has resigned.

Mr Chamberlain was an excellent Minister of Health. He looked after Britain's finances well as Chancellor of the Exchequer. However, some people are worried that he knows so little about foreign affairs.

JAPANESE CAPTURE THE CAPITAL OF CHINA

Dec 13, Nanking, China The Japanese advance goes on. Today their troops entered the Chinese capital Nanking.

NEWS IN BRIEF . . .

GIANT AIRSHIP EXPLODES

May 6, Lakehurst Airfield, USA The giant airship *Hindenburg* fell to the earth in flames tonight, a few metres from the end of its journey across the Atlantic. Watchers on the ground saw a blue flame dart along the airship's back as it drew up to the mooring mast. Seconds later, the two million cubic metres of hydrogen gas that kept the *Hindenburg* aloft caught fire. In a few moments, the airship had become a tangled heap of white-hot metal lying on the ground. It is believed that all 34 people on board have died in the flames.

GREAT COMPOSER DIES

July 11, Hollywood, USA George Gershwin died in a Hollywood hospital today. He was only 38. Gershwin was born in New York. At twenty he was a well-known song-writer. He composed the famous *Rhapsody in Blue* and the music for a string of very successful shows like *Lady be Good, Funny Face* and *Strike up the Band*. America has lost a genius.

JOE LOUIS: HEAVYWEIGHT BOXING CHAMPION

June 3, New York Joe Louis, from Detroit, is the new heavyweight champion of the world. He knocked out the former champion James J. Braddock in the eighth round of their fight. Joe Louis is 23 years old and is the first black boxer to hold the title for 22 years. His nickname is 'The Brown Bomber'.

THE TERROR OF WAR

Oct, Paris, France A painting called *Guernica* has attracted enormous interest at the World Fair in Paris. The artist, Pablo Picasso, is a Spaniard. He painted the picture to protest at the destruction of Guernica by German bombers earlier this year.

Picasso's painting, *Guernica*.

1938

HITLER THREATENS WAR

Sept 27, Germany   Prime Minister Neville Chamberlain has flown to meet Hitler for the second time in a fortnight. Mr Chamberlain hopes face-to-face talks will solve the latest crisis in Europe. Hitler demands that the parts of Czechoslovakia where Germans live should be handed over to Germany. He threatens to take them by force if necessary.

Nazi propaganda poster designed to unite the German people behind Adolf Hitler – "One people, one nation, one leader".

Prime Minister Neville Chamberlain with Adolf Hitler in Munich.

Churchill says, "Don't give in to Hitler"

Sept 28, London   The MP Mr Winston Churchill continues to argue that Mr Chamberlain is wrong to give in to Hitler's demands. He insists that Britain and France should declare that they will fight if the Czechs are attacked. Large crowds attended a meeting in London to back Mr Churchill's stand against Nazi Germany.

Air raid precautions in London: the entrance to a police station is protected by sandbags.

MUNICH MEETING ENDS CRISIS

Neville Chamberlain on his return from Munich with the crowd that greeted him at Heston Airport.

Sept 30, London Joyful crowds welcomed the Prime Minister back from Munich as he landed at Heston aerodrome this evening. Mr Chamberlain thanked the people for their greeting and waved a piece of paper signed by Herr Hitler and himself. It declared that Britain and Germany would never go to war again. "It is peace for our time," he said.

The crisis was ended at a meeting between the leaders of France, Italy and Britain. They agreed that Germany should be allowed to take over the mainly German parts of Czechoslovakia. In return, Hitler has stated there is nothing else he wants from the Czechs, and will leave them in peace. The other leaders have accepted his promise.

There is relief in London but in Prague, the Czech capital, there is anger and dismay. The Czechs claim that Britain and France have betrayed them by giving in to Hitler. They were not even invited to the meeting in Munich that decided their fate.

GERMAN TROOPS INVADE AUSTRIA

March 14, Vienna German troops have crossed the border into Austria. Church bells rang and crowds cheered to welcome Adolf Hitler as he drove through the streets of the Austrian capital, Vienna, today.

The new Austrian Chancellor, Seyss Inquart, is a member of the Nazi Party, and supports Adolf Hitler. He invited the Germans to invade Austria. German is the national language of Austria, and many Austrians would like their country to become part of Germany.

Hitler was born in Austria. Now that his native land is part of Germany he is ruler over 74 million people. Germany has become the most powerful country in Europe.

GERMANS ATTACK AUSTRIAN JEWS

March 18, Vienna   The Germans have lost no time in attacking Jews in Austria. They have issued orders which prevent Jews from being lawyers, doctors or teachers. Jewish shopkeepers and businessmen have been forced to put up notices which say 'Jewish owned' outside their premises.

As part of their increasingly violent campaign against the Jews, the Nazis are smashing Jewish store windows and warning customers away with notices that say "Germans! Defend yourselves! Don't buy from Jews".

Danger of war over Czechoslovakia

May 20, Prague, Czechoslovakia   A dangerous crisis here threatens to plunge Europe and perhaps the world into another war.

German troops now surround Czechoslovakia on three sides. Thousands of Germans live on the Czech side of the border. They claim that the Czech authorities treat them badly and persecute them for being German. Their leaders have appealed to Germany for protection.

If Germany does attack Czechoslovakia it is hard to see how Britain and France could avoid being drawn into the conflict.

FRANCO CLAIMS VICTORY

April 15, Spain   Units of General Franco's army have reached the coast of Spain at Vinaroz. This latest advance by the Nationalists has cut the Republican forces in two. General Franco claims that victory for his side is now certain.

Germans terrorize Jews

Nov 11, Berlin   Two nights ago, all over Germany, mobs set upon the Jews. They burned down synagogues, and attacked and beat up Jews in the streets. Thousands of Jewish shops were broken into and looted. So much shattered glass littered the streets that the Germans are calling the affair "Kristallnacht" – 'the night of broken glass'.

The German government blames it all on the Jews. It claims that the German people turned on them in anger when they heard the news that a Jew had murdered a German diplomat in Paris.

GERMANY ATTACKS CZECHOSLOVAKIA

German-speaking areas of Czechoslovakia

NEWS IN BRIEF . . .

SNOW WHITE AND THE SEVEN DWARFS

Jan, Hollywood Walt Disney's film *Snow White and the Seven Dwarfs* is a huge success. Audiences all over America are flocking to see it. Snow White is the first full-length cartoon film to appear on the screen.

ITALY KEEPS WORLD CUP

June 19, Paris The Italian football team has won the World Cup for the second time. They beat the Hungarians 4–2 in the final here in Paris.

Walt Disney, the creator of Mickey Mouse, has produced another cartoon success with the film *Snow White and the Seven Dwarfs*.

BRITAIN ORDERS 1000 SPITFIRES

July 15, London The British Government has ordered 1000 Spitfires for the Royal Air Force. Experts reckon that the eight-gun Spitfire is the best fighter aircraft in the world today.

CHILDREN GET USED TO THEIR GAS MASKS

Sept 20, London The British Government is providing a free gas mask for every citizen in the country. Children in school have been given practice in wearing their masks. It is feared that bombs containing poison gas would be dropped on Britain, if war were to come.

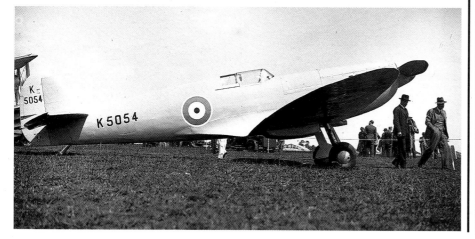

1939

WORLD IN CRISIS
HITLER THREATENS THE CZECHS

March 13, Berlin Hitler has sent a list of demands to the Czech government which they will find impossible to meet. Meanwhile, Nazi newspapers and radio have begun a campaign of hate against the Czech people.

Hitler returned to Berlin last night and received the salutes and cheers from thousands of people following the successful invasion of Czechoslovakia.

GERMANY INVADES CZECHOSLOVAKIA

March 15, Prague German troops have moved into Czechoslovakia. Hitler explains the invasion by claiming that the Czechs have ignored the demands he made on them a few days ago.

Czechs weep as Germans drive through Prague

March 16, Prague Czechs showed anger and bitterness as invading German troops drove through their capital, Prague, today. Some stood silent, some hissed and booed, some shook their fists. Many wept to see their country occupied by a hated enemy. Hitler has boasted publicly, "Czechoslovakia has ceased to exist".

Forced to salute in the Nazi manner, Czechs weep as German soldiers march through the streets of Prague.

CZECH INVASION SHOCKS THE WORLD

March 17, Hitler's take-over of Czechoslovakia has stunned world opinion. Six months after promising at Munich to leave Czechoslovakia in peace, he has seized the country and made it part of Germany. In London, Prime Minister Chamberlain has spoken of his 'shock' at Hitler's action. Both the French and British governments are sending formal notes to Berlin protesting at the German invasion of Czechoslovakia.

HITLER THREATENS POLAND

March 31, Berlin Hitler has now turned against Poland. He demands that the Poles should give up Danzig and return it to Germany. Danzig was once a German city. But it was handed to the Poles after World War I. Hitler also wants the right to build railways and roads across Polish territory, to link Danzig with Germany.

Britain and France have promised to go to Poland's aid if she is attacked by Germany. The three countries will sign a formal treaty next week.

Both France and Britain are building up their military forces as fast as they can. It seems now that war with Germany is certain.

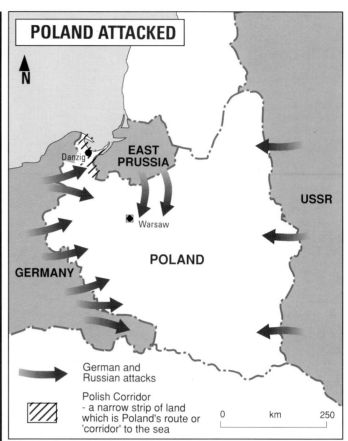

POLAND ATTACKED

→ German and Russian attacks

▨ Polish Corridor - a narrow strip of land which is Poland's route or 'corridor' to the sea

0   km   250

Russia and Germany sign friendship agreement

Aug 23, Moscow Russia and Germany have signed an agreement not to go to war with each other. Britain and France are dismayed by the news. They were hoping to persuade Russia to join them in a pact to protect Poland against an attack by Germany. This surprise agreement means that Hitler can invade Poland without fear of war with Russia.

A gas-proof shelter for animals designed to protect them in an air raid.

EUROPE PREPARES FOR WAR

Aug 31, London Europe is getting ready for war. In Poland, France and Britain, thousands of young men have left their jobs and have been called up to join the armed forces. In Germany, the government has taken over cars, lorries and aircraft for use by the military if war breaks out. Mr Chamberlain has stated again that Britain is bound to go to war, if Poland is attacked.

GERMANY INVADES POLAND

Sept 1, Poland Early this morning, German troops tore down barriers along the Polish border and crossed into Poland. They are advancing rapidly everywhere.

RUSSIA ATTACKS POLAND

Sept 17, Poland Russian troops have invaded Poland. Their aim is to occupy as much of the east of the country before the Germans reach it. The Polish army is trapped and cannot hold out much longer.

BRITAIN AND FRANCE DECLARE WAR ON GERMANY

Sept 3, London Britain and France are at war with Germany. Hitler has not replied to their demand to withdraw his troops from Poland, so war has been declared. Prime Minister Chamberlain gave the news to the British people in a radio broadcast at 11.15 am this morning.

BRITISH TROOPS LAND IN FRANCE

Sept 27, France 150,000 British troops with their equipment and vehicles have landed in France. They are the first part of a larger force that is to follow. The British units will take up positions beside their French allies facing the Germans. Very little fighting has taken place so far.

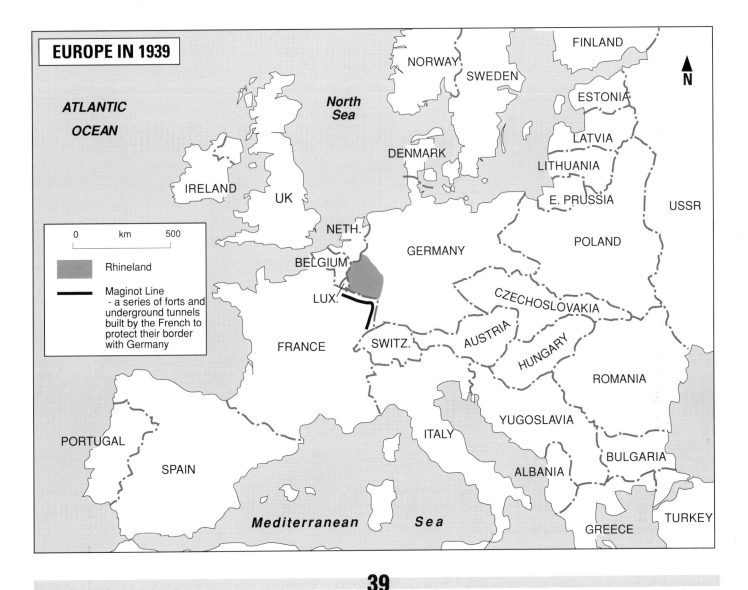

EUROPE IN 1939

FALL OF MADRID ENDS SPANISH CIVIL WAR

March 28, Madrid The Republicans in Madrid have surrendered. General Franco is victorious. The civil war in Spain is over. But Franco faces huge problems. Spain is deeply in debt. Many towns and cities are in ruins and thousands of factories destroyed. Hundreds of thousands of farm animals have died. Trade and industry are at a standstill.

ITALY INVADES ALBANIA

April 8, Rome Yesterday an invasion force of Italian troops landed on the coast of Albania. Today they have occupied the capital Tiranë. King Zog has fled into the country.

The Italian leader Mussolini is jealous of the growing power of Germany. By seizing Albania he is following the lead of his ally Adolf Hitler.

British children moved to safety

Sept 2, London Over 1½ million British children are being evacuated from their homes in the cities to stay with families in the country. The Government fears that the cities will be bombed if war comes. Plans were made some time ago to take city children to safer places, if ever war seemed certain to break out.

NATIONS OF THE WORLD TAKE SIDES

Oct 1, British Commonwealth countries have joined Britain in the war against Germany. The rest of the world, including the United States, is staying neutral.

EVACUATION OF CHILDREN FROM LONDON

Sept 1, "I went to a block of working-class flats at the back of Gray's Inn Road and in the early morning saw a tiny, frail Cockney child walking across to school. The child had a big, brown-paper parcel in her hand and was dragging it along. But as she turned I saw a brown box banging against her thin legs. It bumped up and down at every step, slung by a thin string over her shoulder.

It was Florence Morecombe, an English schoolchild, with a gas mask instead of a satchel over her shoulder.

I went along with Florence to her school. It was a big Council school and the classrooms were filled with children, parcels, gas masks . . . The children were excited and happy because their parents had told them they were going away to the country . . .

I watched the schoolteachers calling out their names and tying luggage labels in their coats, checking their parcels to see there were warm and clean clothes . . . mothers and fathers were saying goodbye, straightening the girls' hair, getting the boys to blow their noses and lightly and quickly kissing them . . . There was quite a long wait before this small army got its orders . . . to move off . . .

Labelled and lined up the children began to move out of the school."

(Hilde Marchant, *Women and Children Last*, Victor Gollancz Ltd, 1941)

British victory at the battle of the River Plate

Dec 17, Montevideo, Uruguay The German pocket battleship *Graf Spee* has sunk. She was blown up by her own crew. British warships were lying in wait as the *Graf Spee* left Montevideo harbour. There was no way of escape, so the German crew sent her to the bottom. For weeks the Royal Navy has been searching the seas for the *Graf Spee*. This victory will do much to lift British spirits.

The *Graf Spee* sinks in the estuary of the River Plate. Following the recent losses of the aircraft carrier *Courageous* and the battleship *Royal Oak* this victory will do much to raise British spirits.

NEWS IN BRIEF . . .

NEW WONDER FABRIC 'NYLON' HITS THE SHOPS

Feb 21, New York Women's stockings made of nylon have gone on sale for the first time. They cost $1.15 a pair. Nylon looks and feels like silk but is much cheaper, washes more easily and lasts longer. Other garments made of nylon are on the way. Women's underwear and men's shirts will follow soon.

TELEVISION ARRIVES IN USA

April 30, New York America's first regular television service made its first broadcast today! Television cameras filmed President Roosevelt as he opened New York's World's Fair.

FIRST PASSENGER FLIGHTS ACROSS THE ATLANTIC

June 28, Southampton Pan American Airways have begun regular passenger flights across the Atlantic. The service will be operated by Boeing flying boats. The first aircraft to make the flight from Newfoundland landed safely on Southampton Water this afternoon.

Pan American Airways are using the Boeing 314 flying-boat *Yankee Clipper* for their new transatlantic passenger flights.

PEOPLE OF THE THIRTIES

Neville Chamberlain 1869–1940

British Prime Minister. Chamberlain entered Parliament in 1918 as a member of the Tory, or Conservative, Party. He became Prime Minister in 1937. Chamberlain knew little about foreign affairs and Hitler was able to fool him completely over the Czech crisis (see page 38). He took Britain into the war in 1939, but resigned in 1940. He died of cancer six months later.

Marie Curie, Polish/French scientist 1867–1934

Marie Curie was Polish but moved to France to study science. There she married a scientist, Pierre Curie. Together they studied the strange rays given off by the metal uranium. After Pierre died Marie continued their work. In 1911 she received a Nobel Prize for discoveries in radioactivity which are vital to the cure for cancer. She died of a blood disorder caused by the radioactivity which made her famous. (See page 23.)

Walt Disney, American film-maker 1901–1966

Walt Disney has probably done more to entertain people than anyone who has ever lived. His most famous creation was Mickey Mouse. Mickey first appeared in 1928, and in the thirties was joined by Minnie Mouse, Donald Duck, Goofy, Pluto and a cast of other characters which are known and loved around the world. Disney went on to produce full-length cartoons and adventure films. (See page 36.)

Francisco Franco 1892–1975

Spanish dictator. Franco organized the revolt against the government which set off the Spanish civil war. He ended the war as head of state in Spain. He ruled Spain as a dictator from 1937 until his death in 1975. (See page 40.)

Mahatma Gandhi 1869–1948

Indian independence leader. Gandhi trained as a lawyer. After World War I he became leader of the movement to end British rule in India. He persuaded his followers to defy British laws, but never to use violence. Millions followed his example of peaceful disobedience. India won independence in 1948, but a religious fanatic murdered Gandhi a few months later. (See page 16.)

George Gershwin, American composer 1898–1937

George Gershwin's parents were Russian Jews who had come to live in New York City. Young George loved music but was too poor to pay for lessons, so he taught himself. His song *Swanee* made him famous before he was twenty. George wrote the music for many successful stage shows and films. (See page 32.)

Adolf Hitler 1889–1945

Hitler was born in Austria, but moved to Germany. In 1933 he became dictator of Germany. He seized Austria and Czechoslovakia and, in 1939, invaded Poland. World War II followed. Hitler won many victories at first, but was finally defeated by the combined forces of Russia, America and Britain. He killed himself in 1945, as the Russians entered Berlin.

Benito Mussolini 1883–1945

Italian dictator. Mussolini was a teacher and then a journalist. He entered politics and became leader of the Fascist Party. In 1922 he became Prime Minister of Italy. He got rid of those who opposed him and by 1929 had become an all-powerful dictator. In 1935 he seized Abyssinia. He became Hitler's ally in World War II, but was defeated in 1943. He was shot by Italian freedom fighters in 1945. (See page 40.)

Pablo Picasso, Spanish artist 1881–1973

Pablo Picasso was a Spaniard, but moved to Paris in 1904. He spent the rest of his life in France where he produced a huge variety of paintings, drawings, prints and sculptures. His work had a powerful influence on other artists of his time. The painting *Guernica* (see page 32) was Picasso's protest at the cruelty and horror of the civil war in Spain.

Franklin D. Roosevelt 1882–1945

President of the United States. Roosevelt was crippled by polio and could not stand or walk without help. In spite of this, he was elected President. In the 1930s, his New Deal policy rescued America from the world economic depression. He led the USA into World War II in 1941, against Germany and Japan. In 1944 he became President for a record fourth time, but died in April 1945 just before victory. (See page 27.)

Joseph Stalin 1879–1953

Communist dictator. Stalin was a leader of the revolution of 1917 in Russia, which put the Communists in power. He got rid of everyone who stood in his way, and became sole dictator. Russia was then very backward. Stalin brought it up to date. Those who opposed the changes 'disappeared'. Millions died on his orders. In World War II, Stalin led Russia to victory over Nazi Germany. (See page 25.)

Mao Tse-Tung 1893–1976

First leader of Communist China. In 1921 the Chinese Communist party was founded. Mao was one of those who set it up. In 1934–35 he led the Long March of the Communist army through all opposition to a safe place in northern China. After World War II he defeated the Nationalists under Chiang Kai-Shek, and made China into a Communist state. (See page 25.)

For the first time ever

1930	USA	Frozen food on sale to the public. Process invented by Clarence Birdseye
		Carrothers discovers Nylon
1931	USA	First long-playing record released
	Germany	Electron microscope built
1932	USA	First domestic air-conditioner produced
		First artificial heart pace-maker developed
		First yellow fever vaccine developed
1933	UK	Polythene produced
1934	UK	Cat's-eye road studs first used
		Driving tests introduced
	Germany	First successful radar demonstration
1935	USA	First parking meters installed
		First public launderette opened
	UK	Radar used to detect aircraft
	Germany	First tape recorder on sale called the Magnetophone
1936	Germany	First practical helicopter demonstration
1937	USA	First electric blanket on sale
		Radio telescopes built
	UK	Whittle's jet engine successfully tested

1938	USA	Xerox copier appeared
		Nylon manufactured
		Breathalyser introduced
		Teflon produced
	Hungary	Ball point pen (Biro) invented
1939	Switzerland	DDT first used
	Germany	First jet aircraft test flight
		Successful splitting of the atom
	USA	Fluorescent lighting used

New words and expressions

The English language is always changing. New words are added to it, and old words are used in new ways. Here are a few of the words and expressions that appeared for the first time in the 1930s:

air-raid	jet-propelled
air-conditioned	jittery
ammo	motivate
antisocial	microfilm
binge	Nazi
bomb-load	newscaster
bomb-sight	nylon and nylons
bottle party	old school tie
Brains Trust	perspex
build-up	playpen
bulldozer	powder compact
coolant	quickie
don't be funny!	raw deal
doodle	scram!
drop dead!	slap up
folding money	spiv
fridge	step on the gas
gift-coupon	tailor-made
go-slow	whistlestop
jam session	whodunit

How many of these words and expressions do we still use today? Do you know what they all mean?

Glossary

Abyssinia: a country in north-east Africa now called Ethiopia.

Chancellor: head of the government in Germany and Austria.

Chancellor of the Exchequer: in Britain, the Government minister in charge of the country's finances.

Communism: a political theory. Communists believe that all property and industry in a country should belong to the State.

concentration camps: During the Boer War 1899–1902 the British set up internment camps to hold the families of Boer commando fighters. These camps became known as 'concentration camps'. The Nazis borrowed this term for the camps they built to imprison enemies of the state.

dictator: a ruler who has total power in his own country, for example Hitler, Stalin and Mussolini.

diplomat: an official sent abroad to represent his country to another government.

gulag: a prison camp in Soviet Russia.

kulak: a Russian peasant who owned land.

League of Nations: the international organization set up after World War I to keep peace between nations and solve world problems by discussion.

Mahatma: an Indian title meaning 'great and wise' for example, Mahatma Gandhi.

Nationalists: In Spain, the party which supported strong central government by a dictator led by General Franco.

Nazi: the short form in German of 'The National Socialist German Workers' Party'

New Deal: President Roosevelt's programme, in 1933, for rebuilding the American economy after the slump. He called it a 'New Deal' for America.

Nobel Prize: given to people who have done something very important for world peace, or in science or literature.

Prime Minister: the head of the Government in Great Britain.

Reichstag: the German parliament and the building it met in.

Republic: a country in which the Head of State (usually a President) is chosen by vote.

Republicans: (also known as the Popular Front) In Spain the party of the Socialists, Trade Unions and those who stood for a government elected by the votes of the people.

slump: the worldwide economic problems and unemployment of the early 1930s. Also called the 'Great Depression'.

synagogue: a building in which Jews hold religious sevices.

Versailles Treaty: the treaty of 1919, named after the palace near Paris where it was signed, that ended World War I.

Further Reading

The Twentieth Century World: Peter and Mary Speed. Oxford University Press 1982

Working with Evidence: The Modern World: Peter and Mary Speed. Oxford University Press 1985

Rainbow Fact Book of the Twentieth Century: George Beal. Kingfisher 1985

Britain Between the World Wars 1918–1939: Marion Yass. Wayland 1975

A Family in the Thirties: Sue Crawford. Wayland 1989

Great Lives: Simon Boughton. Kingfisher 1988

Gandhi: Catherine Bush. Burke 1985

Hitler and the Third Reich: Catherine Bradley. Watts 1990

Roosevelt and the United States: O. B. O'Callaghan. Longmans 1966

Russia under Stalin: Michael Gibson. Wayland 1972

Index